This Book Belongs to:

_____

SEDUCTIVE SAYINGS

MARILYN MONROE
HER OWN WORDS
ON SEX, FAME, HOLLYWOOD,
AND MARILYN

LONGMEADOW PRESS

Jacket design by Lisa Amoroso
Interior design by Lisa Amoroso
Interior photos by PHOTOFEST

ISBN: 0-681-45364-8
Printed in Singapore
First Edition
0 9 8 7 6 5 4 3 2 1

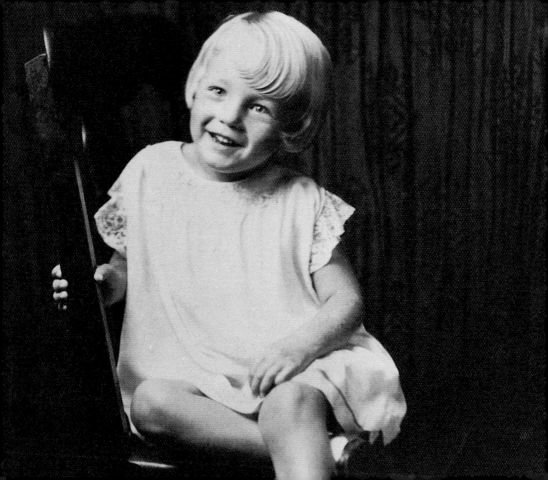

Acting is a feminine art.

I used to think as I looked out on the Hollywood night, "There must be thousands of girls sitting alone like me dreaming of becoming a movie star. But I'm not going to worry about them. I'm dreaming the hardest."

A man with perfect teeth always alienated me. I don't know what it is but it has something to do with the kind of men I have known who had perfect teeth. They weren't so perfect elsewhere.

Husbands are chiefly good as lovers when they are betraying their wives.

The truth is I've never fooled anyone. I've let men sometimes fool themselves.

I always felt I was a nobody, and the only way for me to be somebody – was to be somebody else.

I've tried almost everything – at least once.

I sometimes feel as if I'm too exposed. I've given myself away, the whole of me, every part, and there's nothing left that's private, just me alone.

Joe DiMaggio was the best equipped.   The greatest.
If our marriage was only sex, it would last forever.

Nobody ever got cancer from sex.

You can't sleep your way into being a star . . .
but it helps.

Frank Sinatra is the most fascinating man I ever
dated. When I'm with him, I feel like I don't have to
take pills.

It was wonderful being a girl, but it's more wonderful being a woman.

I've spent most of my life running away from myself.

I was never kept; I always kept myself.

This is the end of my story of Norma Jean. I moved into a room in Hollywood to live by myself. I was nineteen, and I wanted to find out who I was.

Hollywood's a place where they will pay you a thousand dollars for a kiss, and fifty cents for your soul.

Being a movie star was never as much fun as dreaming of being one.

When you're a failure in Hollywood — that's like starving to death outside a banquet hall with the smells of filet mignon driving you crazy.

A career is wonderful, but you can't curl up with a career on a cold night.

Arthur Miller is a wonderful writer, a brilliant man.
But I think he is a better writer than a husband.

It's better to be unhappy alone than unhappy with
someone.

I never quite understood it – this sex symbol – I always thought symbols were those things you clash together.

A movie job hunter without a car in Hollywood was like a fireman without a fire engine.

It is hard to explain how much you can fall in love while you are being bored to death, but I know it's true, because it happened to me several times.

If I'd observed all the rules, I'd never have got anywhere.

Everybody is always tugging at you. They'd all like
to take pieces out of you.

As far as I'm concerned there's a future and I can't
wait to get to it.

M A R I L Y N

I belonged to the public and to the world, not because I was talented or even beautiful but because I had never belonged to anything or anyone else.

I am not interested in money. I just want to be wonderful.

M O N R O E

Marilyn Monroe has to look a certain way – be beautiful – and act a certain way, be talented. I wondered if I could live up to their expectations.

In Hollywood they never ask me my opinion. They just tell me what time to come to work.

M A R I L Y N

Sometimes I'm invited places to brighten up a dinner table, like a musicican who'll play the piano after dinner. You're not really invited for yourself, you're just an ornament.

A struggle with shyness is in every actor more than anyone can imagine.

M O N R O E

When you don't want a lover, all kinds of
opportunities come your way.

I think that sexuality is only attractive when it's
natural and spontaneous.

I don't mind making jokes but I don't want to look like one.

The worst thing that happens to people when they dress up and go to a party is that they leave their real selves at home.

Wives have a tendency to go off like burglar alarms when they see their husbands talking to me.

The chief difference between my voice and the voices of most women I've seen is that I use mine less.

The real lover is the man who can thrill you by just touching your head or smiling into your eyes – or by just staring into space.

I've always been attracted to men who wore glasses.

MONROE

Being late is a desire not to be there.

When a man says to me, "I'm giving you exactly the same advice I'd give my own daughter," I know he isn't "dangerous" anymore – that is, if he actually has a daughter.

I don't mind this being a man's world — as long as I can be a woman in it.

Most men judge your importance in their lives by how much you can hurt them, not by how happy you can make them.

Love is something you can't invent, no matter how much you want to.

I've come to love that line "until death do us part." It always seems to go well for a time, and then something happens. Maybe it's me.

In Hollywood, the more important a man is the more he talks. The better he is at his job the more he brags.

In Hollywood, a girl's virtue is much less important than her hair-do.

Yes, there was something special about me, and I knew what it was. I was the kind of girl they found dead in a hall bedroom with an empty bottle of sleeping pills in her hand.

I sometimes felt I was hooked on sex, the way an alcoholic is on liquor or a junkie on dope.

Sometimes I've been to a party where no one spoke to me a whole evening. The men, frightened by their wives or sweeties, would give me a wide berth. And the ladies would gang up in a corner to discuss my dangerous character.

I always keep my undies in the icebox.

MARILYN

I'm only comfortable when I'm naked.

As soon as I could afford an evening gown, I bought
the loudest one I could find. It was a bright red,
low-cut dress, and my arrival in it usually infuriated
half the women present. I was sorry in a way to do
this, but I had a long way to go, and I needed a lot of
advertising to get there.

MONROE

The dark star I was born under was going to get darker and darker.

Kindness is the strangest thing to find in a lover – or in anybody.